# What Does a Book Designer Do?



In this book, Sarah uses the jargon of a book designer. Jargon words are explained in boxes like the one below:

**JARGON**

Jargon: the words and phrases that mean special things in a job

## Contents



Trackers

# Meet Sarah

Hi, I'm Sarah. I'm a book designer. I take the words someone has written and make a book out of them.

My rubber plant
Big screen!
Reference books
I bike to work.
Clip art CDs
Back rest. Sitting correctly is very important when you work at a computer all day.

## JARGON

Clip art: little pictures to use on pages

# The People I Work With

**JARGON**

Editor: the person who reviews something someone else has written, suggesting changes and ways to make it better

**JARGON**

Author: the person who writes the book

**JARGON**

Art: all the drawings or photos that go into a book

I spend most of my time alone working at my computer. It takes lots of people to make a book, though!

# Starting the Design

Here's how I designed a book called *It's Magic!*.

*It's Magic!* was edited before I saw it. The editor sent me an email with the **manuscript**.

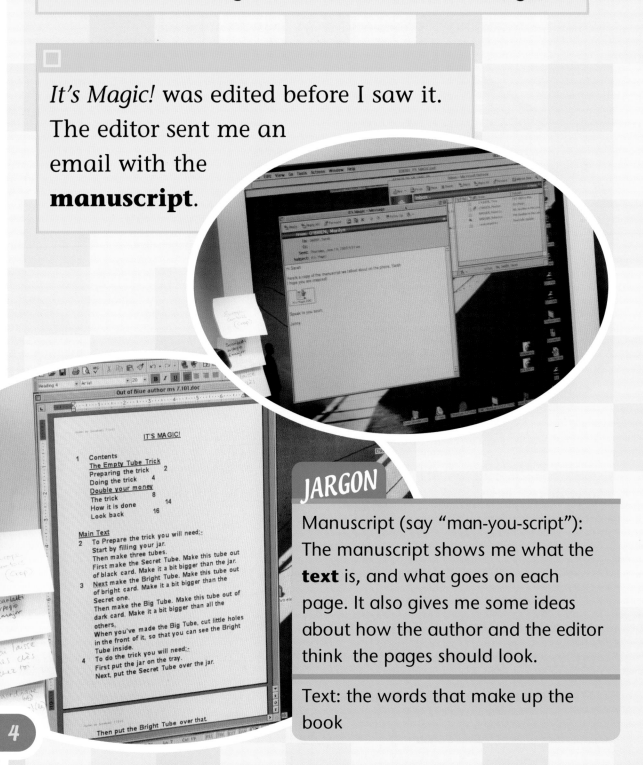

It's Magic - Message
From: O'BRIEN, Marilyn

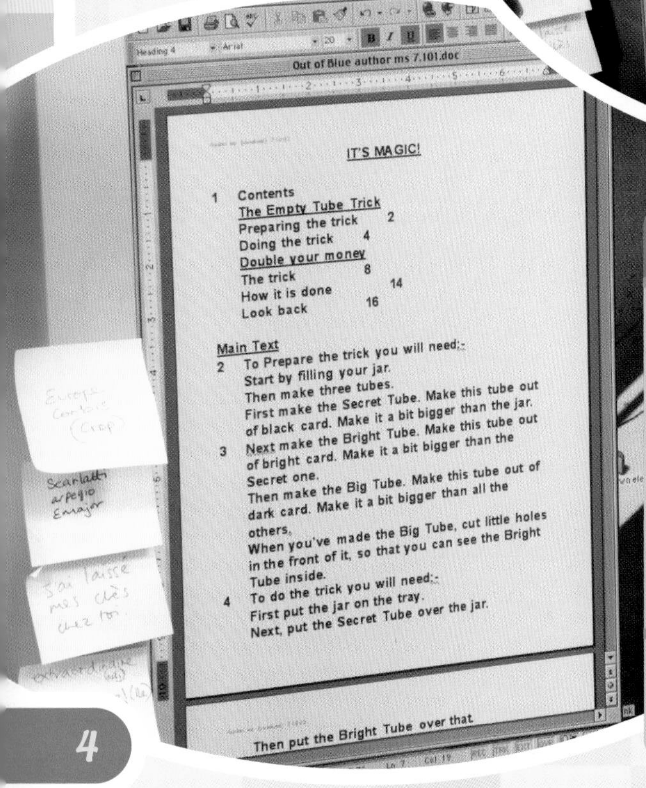

Out of Blue author ms 7.101.doc
IT'S MAGIC!
1 Contents
The Empty Tube Trick
Preparing the trick 2
Doing the trick 4
Double your money
The trick 8
How it is done 14
Look back 16
Main Text
2 To Prepare the trick you will need:-
Start by filling your jar.
Then make three tubes.
First make the Secret Tube. Make this tube out of black card. Make it a bit bigger than the jar.
3 Next make the Bright Tube. Make this tube out of bright card. Make it a bit bigger than the Secret one.
Then make the Big Tube. Make this tube out of dark card. Make it a bit bigger than all the others.
When you've made the Big Tube, cut little holes in the front of it, so that you can see the Bright Tube inside.
4 To do the trick you will need:-
First put the jar on the tray.
Next, put the Secret Tube over the jar.
Then put the Bright Tube over that

## JARGON

Manuscript (say "man-you-script"): The manuscript shows me what the **text** is, and what goes on each page. It also gives me some ideas about how the author and the editor think the pages should look.

Text: the words that make up the book

I read the manuscript. I needed to know:

- what the book was about,
- who the book was for,
- what the book was trying to do.

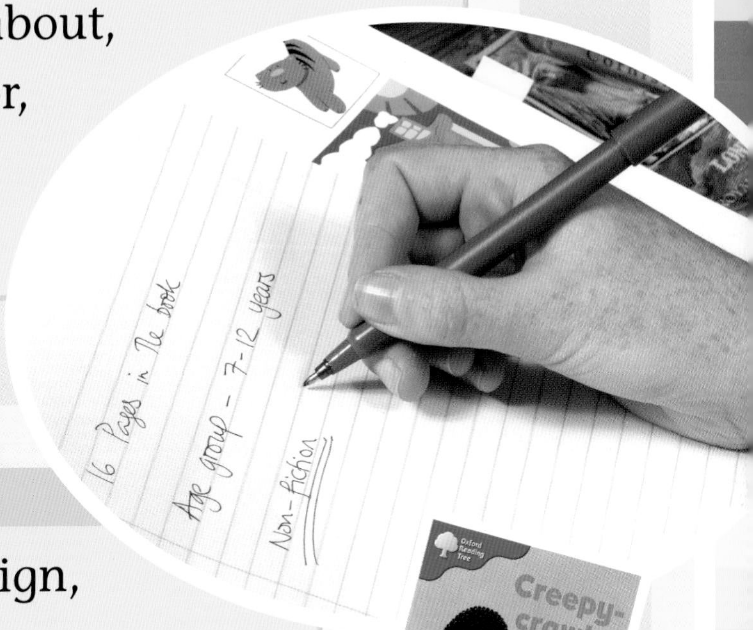


Before I started my design, I also needed to know:

- the number of pages in the book,
- the size of the pages,
- if the book was going to be in color or black and white,
- what sizes and shapes the **fonts** needed to be.

## JARGON

Font: the shape of the letters in a book. Fonts can be all kinds of shapes.

*Some fonts are curly like this.*

**Some are thick like this.**

Who do you think these books have been designed for?

# Creating a Background

This book was about magic tricks. I wanted to design this book to look magical. I thought about magic. I got ideas from:

- books,
- the internet,
- magazines,
- TV.

This book was going to be in color and for children, so I could make a fun background. I made three background designs.

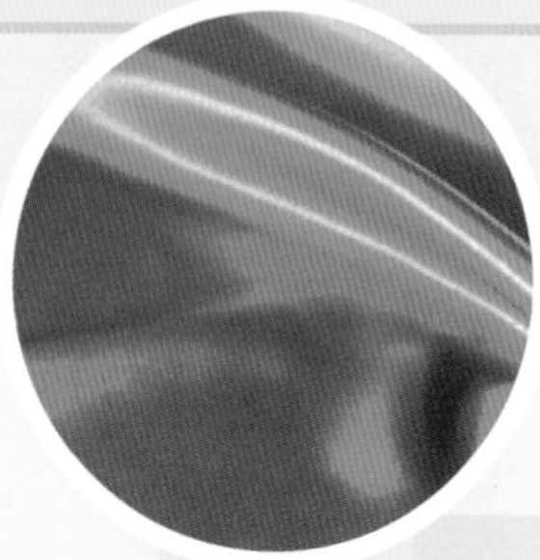

Which would you choose?

# ... Page

... to
... t
... nd out.

... igned a magician's
... for the **folios**.

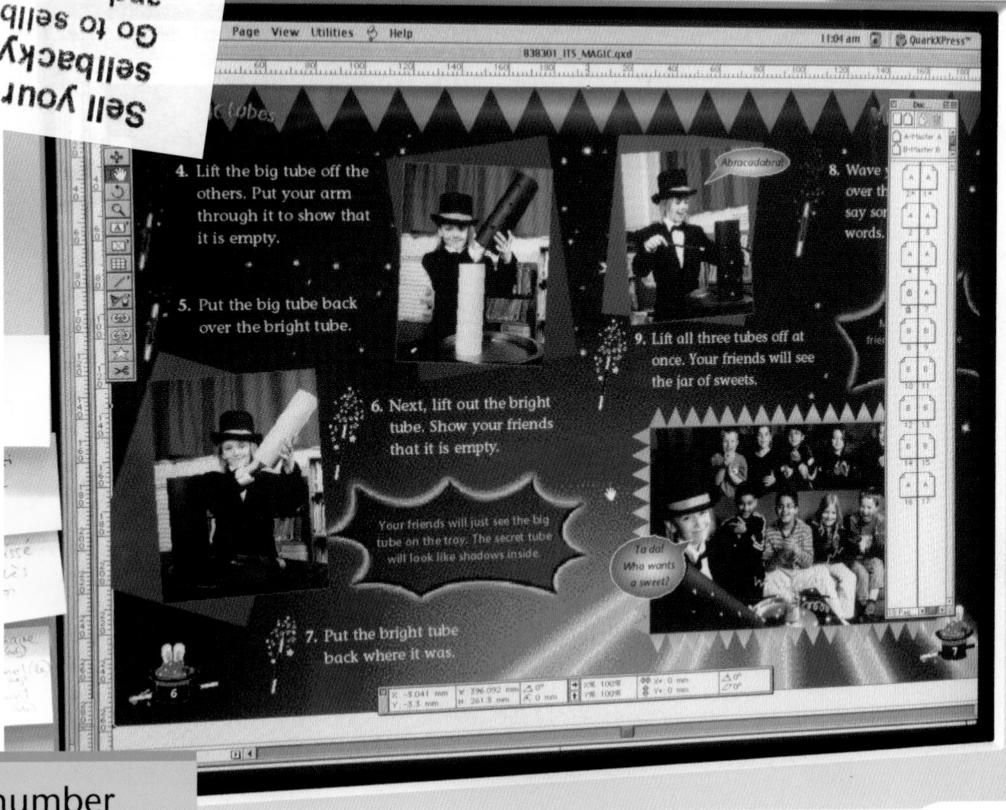
Page View Utilities Help
4. Lift the big tube off the others. Put your arm through it to show that it is empty.
5. Put the big tube back over the bright tube.
6. Next, lift out the bright tube. Show your friends that it is empty.
7. Put the bright tube back where it was.
9. Lift all three tubes off at once. Your friends will see the jar of sweets.
Abracadabra!
Your friends will just see the big tube on the tray. The secret tube will look like shadows inside.
Ta da! Who wants a sweet?

**JARGON**

folio: a page number

# The First Layout

I chose this background for the book because it has a strong feeling of magic, and the dark color is unusual.

Blocks of color show where pictures will go. Notes in the blocks say what the photo should look like when it is taken.

I made a layout of one **spread** to show to the author and the editors.

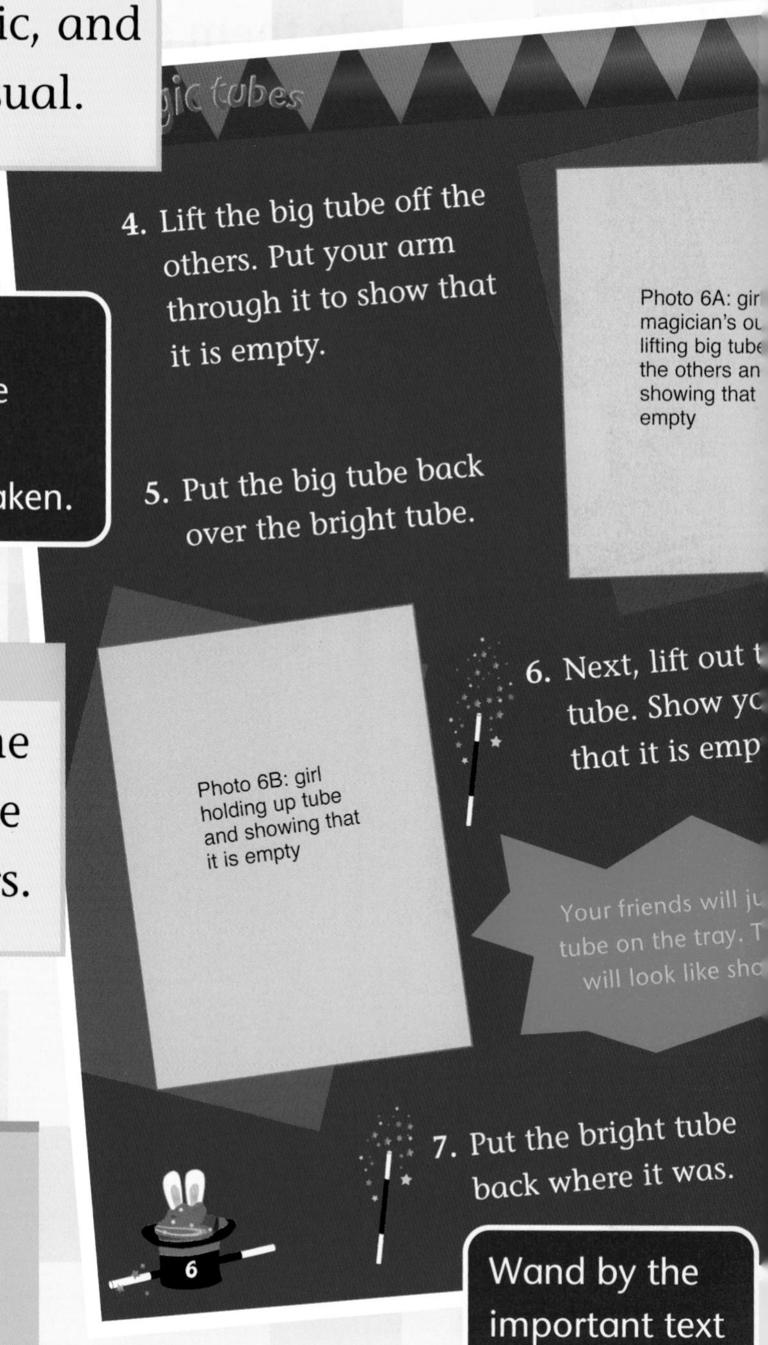
4. Lift the big tube off the others. Put your arm through it to show that it is empty.
5. Put the big tube back over the bright tube.
Photo 6B: girl holding up tube and showing that it is empty
7. Put the bright tube back where it was.
6

Wand by the important text

## JARGON

Spread: a pair of pages that are side by side. The spread shown here is made of pages 6 and 7 from *It's Magic!*.

## JARGON

Layout: a full-size example of what pages will look like

I cut and pasted text from the manuscript to put on my background.

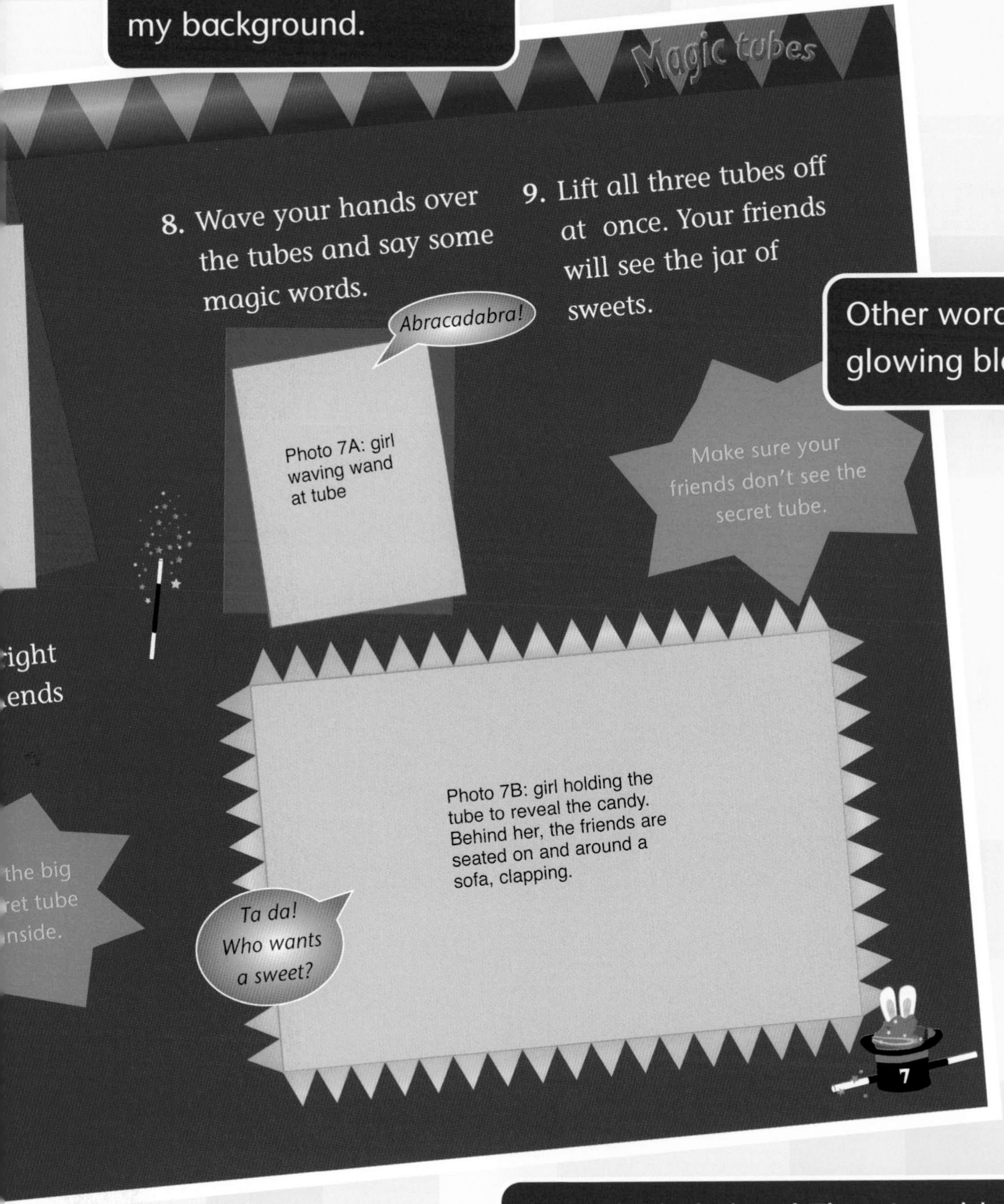

Magic tubes
8. Wave your hands over the tubes and say some magic words.
9. Lift all three tubes off at once. Your friends will see the jar of sweets.
Abracadabra!
Photo 7A: girl waving wand at tube
Make sure your friends don't see the secret tube.
Photo 7B: girl holding the tube to reveal the candy. Behind her, the friends are seated on and around a sofa, clapping.
Ta da! Who wants a sweet?
7

Other words in glowing blocks

They liked it! Phew! Then I could make **layouts** of the whole book.

# Changes

Author: This text needs to be read before this picture. Can you switch them ?
Editor: Can you make this picture bigger?

The author and editors looked at my layouts. They liked them, but they wanted to make some small changes.

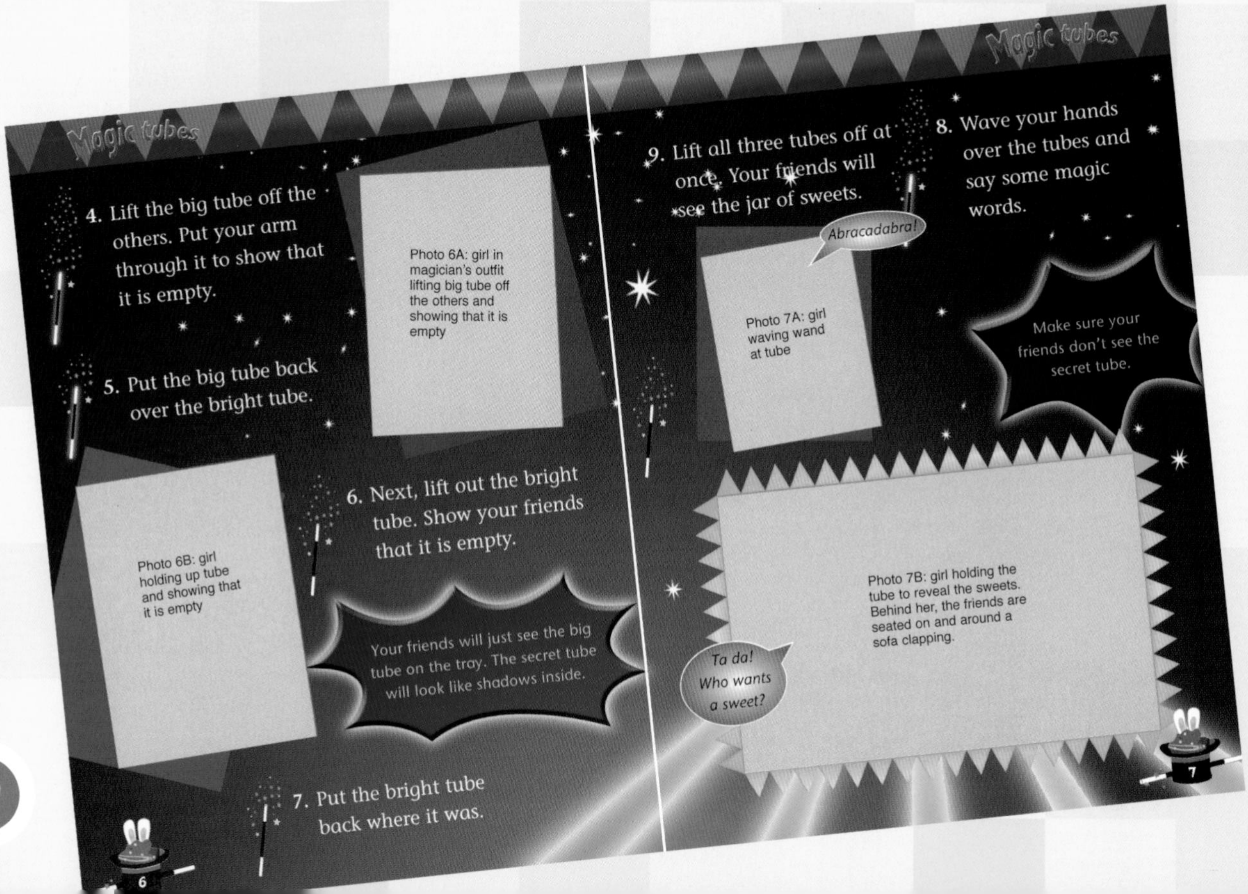
Magic tubes
4. Lift the big tube off the others. Put your arm through it to show that it is empty.
Photo 6A: girl in magician's outfit lifting big tube off the others and showing that it is empty
5. Put the big tube back over the bright tube.
Photo 6B: girl holding up tube and showing that it is empty
6. Next, lift out the bright tube. Show your friends that it is empty.
Your friends will just see the big tube on the tray. The secret tube will look like shadows inside.
7. Put the bright tube back where it was.
6
Magic tubes
9. Lift all three tubes off at once. Your friends will see the jar of sweets.
8. Wave your hands over the tubes and say some magic words.
Abracadabra!
Photo 7A: girl waving wand at tube
Make sure your friends don't see the secret tube.
Photo 7B: girl holding the tube to reveal the sweets. Behind her, the friends are seated on and around a sofa clapping.
Ta da! Who wants a sweet?
7

I went back and made the changes. The group looked at them again and again!

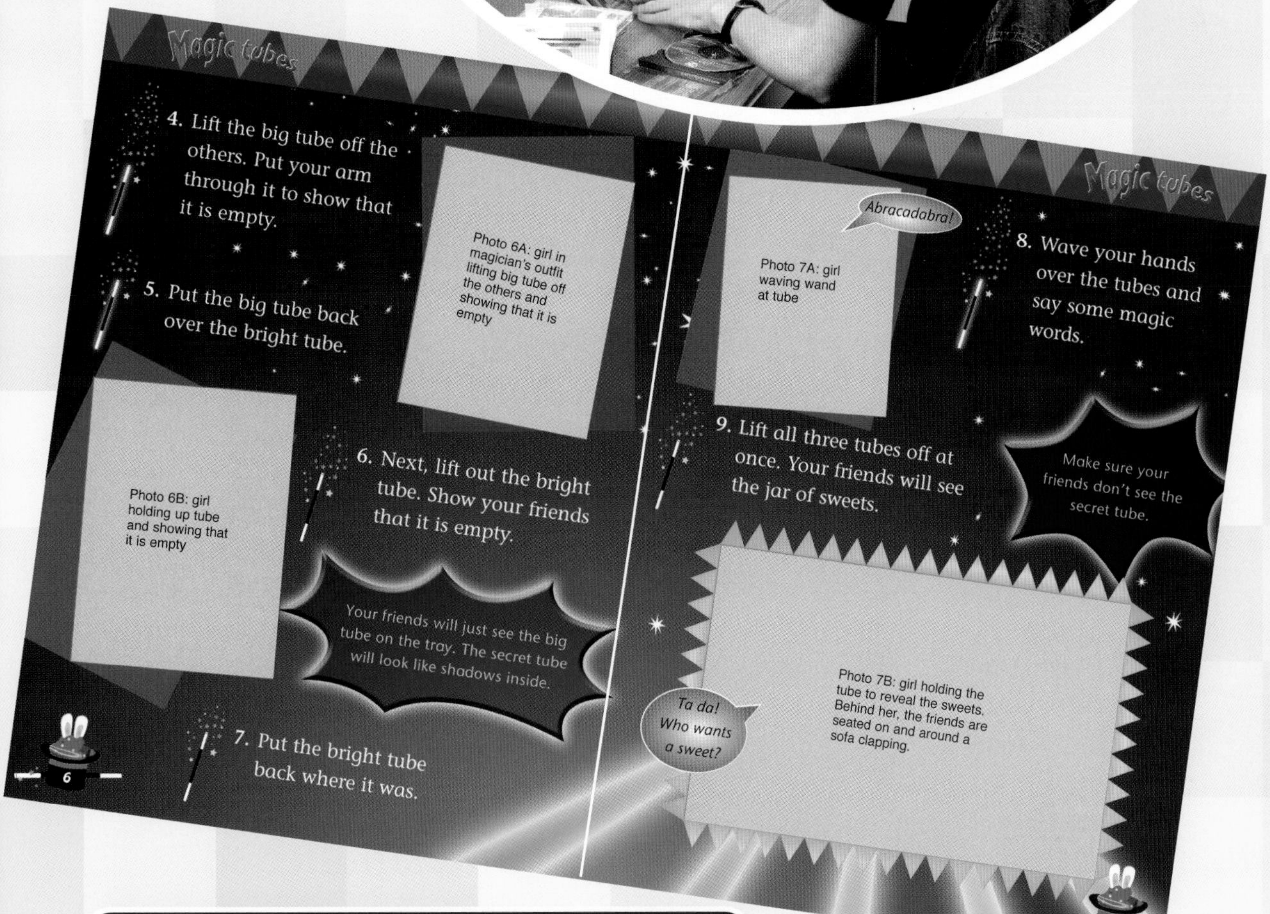

Magic tubes

4. Lift the big tube off the others. Put your arm through it to show that it is empty.

5. Put the big tube back over the bright tube.

Photo 6A: girl in magician's outfit lifting big tube off the others and showing that it is empty

Photo 6B: girl holding up tube and showing that it is empty

6. Next, lift out the bright tube. Show your friends that it is empty.

Your friends will just see the big tube on the tray. The secret tube will look like shadows inside.

7. Put the bright tube back where it was.

6

Magic tubes

Abracadabra!

Photo 7A: girl waving wand at tube

8. Wave your hands over the tubes and say some magic words.

9. Lift all three tubes off at once. Your friends will see the jar of sweets.

Make sure your friends don't see the secret tube.

Ta da! Who wants a sweet?

Photo 7B: girl holding the tube to reveal the sweets. Behind her, the friends are seated on and around a sofa clapping.

7

I made three layouts before everyone agreed that it was right.

# The Photo Shoot

I went with the art editor and a photographer to take photos for the book.

We asked a local student to be our model.

When I got back to my desk, I loaded the pictures onto my computer. Then I put them into the layouts. I made them bigger and smaller so they would fit into the spaces I had left for them.

# The Cover

The cover is very important. It can make people want to read the book. There was a special meeting about the cover. I took three covers with me to the meeting. Everyone decided which cover was best for the book.

This one looks exciting.
I don't like this font.
This one won't sell.
It's Magic!
OXFORD
Sarah Fleming

I had a favorite. I tried to get everyone to choose my favorite!

Which one would you choose?

# Production

When everything was ready, I put the book onto a CD. Then I gave the book to the **production** manager. He made **proofs** of the pages.

2. Say that you have two magic tubes on your tray.
3. Say that the magic tubes are empty now, but they won't be for long...
Magic tubes
Abracadabra!
8. Wave your hands over the tubes and say some magic words.
9. Lift all three tubes off at once. Your friends will see the jar of sweets.
Your friends will just see the big tube on the tray. The secret tube will look like shadows inside.
7. Put the bright tube back where it was.
Ta da! Who wants a sweet?

## JARGON

Production: taking the CD of book design and making it into a real book

The editors and I checked the proofs for mistakes. This was the last time we would be able to change anything. When the proofs were correct, the book was printed.

## JARGON

Proofs: printouts that show what the pages will look like

# The Result

Whose book is this now?

- The designer's?
- The author's?
- The editor's?
- The reader's?

It's taken more than eighteen months to make this book. Now we have to see if readers like it!

# My Job: The Good and Bad Things

**Good**

- I like creating designs and inventing new looks on the computer.
- I like taking the puzzle of a page of words and art and making it into a good layout.
- I like seeing the book when it is finished.

**Bad**

- I don't like going to meetings!
- I don't like having to make changes to my designs.
- If the book is a simple black-and-white textbook, designing it can be boring.

# How I Became a Book Designer

I studied fine arts in college. Then I traveled around the world and lived in another country for two years. After that, I joined a publishing company, but I didn't start as a designer. While I was working there I taught myself to use the computer programs that book designers use. I applied for a design job, and I was hired. My fine arts degree helps me to understand how to make pages look interesting. A lot of book designers study design in college.